Contents

Let's celebrate! 2

Australian celebrations 4

I won't forget 7

How to organise a Harmony Day celebration 10

The Lion Drummer 13

Strands in action 16

Let's celebrate!

Celebration is a kind of food we all need in our lives, and each individual brings a special recipe or offering, so that together we will make a great feast.

Corita Kent and Jan Steward, artists

Celebrations and **commemorations** are special. They're not something we do every day. We have them to remember important **events**.

Most of us get together with family and friends to celebrate occasions such as birthdays. Sometimes we join with people in our community to celebrate events such as grand finals. We may also commemorate events such as Anzac Day.

Celebrations and commemorations are things we do with other people. We talk, share food or share memories. These things are an important part of life.

Did you know?

You can see fireworks before you hear them. That's because light travels faster than sound. When you see fireworks, count the seconds until you hear the noise. Divide by three to work out how many kilometres are between you and the fireworks.

commemorations events for remembering a person or something that happened in the past

events occasions that happen

Fireworks are often part of celebrations.

LET'S FIND OUT

- What special events do we celebrate?
- Why do people celebrate together?
- What celebrations from other countries are part of Australian life?
- Why is NAIDOC Week important?
- Why is Anzac Day important?

Australian celebrations

Celebrations are part of the Australian way of life. Many people celebrate special family events. Other celebrations are special to the whole country.

Australia Day

Australia's **national** day is celebrated on 26 January. On this day in 1788, people arrived on the **First Fleet** to start new lives here. Many Aboriginal and Torres Strait Islander people do not celebrate this day.

Australia Day celebrations include barbecues, playing sport and going to the beach. Some people put Australian flags on their cars and houses – or paint them on their faces!

There are **ceremonies** for people who want to become Australians. Special awards are given to people who have done something brave or important.

national about a nation or a country
First Fleet the first group of ships that brought people from Britain to Australia
ceremonies official or formal parts of important events

Harmony Day

Harmony Day is held to celebrate that people from many countries can live together in Australia. Everyone shows understanding for all the different **traditions**.

NAIDOC Week

NAIDOC Week is held to celebrate the lives of Australia's Aboriginal and Torres Strait Islander people. Traditions are celebrated, as well as ways of living now.

Children in traditional dress at a NAIDOC Week parade in northern Queensland

Conclusion

Getting together for celebrations helps people understand each other and be proud of their country.

---

harmony when everyone gets along with each other

traditions ways of doing things that are passed on from adults to children

NAIDOC National Aborigines and Islanders Day Observance Committee

Breakaway tasks

Remembering

1 Make a list of ways people celebrate on Australia Day.

Understanding

2 Why is Australia Day on 26 January?
3 Explain what we celebrate on Harmony Day.
4 Explain what we celebrate during NAIDOC Week.

Applying

5 Make a timeline of all the events that your family celebrates every year.

Analysing

6 Write down some reasons why Aboriginal and Torres Strait Islander people might not celebrate Australia Day.
7 Choose one Australian celebration. Research and write about why it is special.

Evaluating

8 Which Australian celebration do you think is the most important? Give your reasons.
9 With a partner, talk about why getting together for Australian celebrations is an important part of our way of life.

Creating

10 Create a poster for a celebration in your community. Include pictures and a description.

I won't forget

On Anzac Day we commemorate the men and women who went to wars to fight for our country. My grandma goes to the Anzac Day march every year. This year, Grandma has asked me to go with her.

Interview of Janet Brown by her grandson, Zac Brown

ZB: Grandma, why do you march in the Anzac Day parade?

JB: Well, I do it in memory of your grandpa. He was a soldier in the Vietnam War in 1969.

ZB: What happened to Grandpa in Vietnam?

JB: He was in a big battle. Grandpa got a medal for saving another soldier.

ZB: I didn't know Grandpa was a hero. He must have been very brave. Did Grandpa march in the parade every year?

JB: Yes, he did. He wanted to remember his mates and his grandpa, your great-great-grandpa, who was a soldier in the First World War. He was an Anzac.

ZB: We learnt about the Anzacs at school. 'Anzac' stands for Australian and New Zealand Army **Corps**. They were the soldiers who landed at Gallipoli in Turkey on 25 April 1915. It was a terrible battle and the soldiers were very brave.

JB: That's right. The Anzac story is an important part of our history.

ZB: Why did you ask me to march with you this year, Grandma?

JB: I want you to learn about your grandpa's **legacy**; he helped to keep our country safe. And you can wear his medals. They're getting too heavy for me now!

corps a main part of a large group of soldiers
legacy something that's passed on

Breakaway tasks

Remembering

1 List the places Zac's grandpa and great-great-grandpa went to fight.

2 What does 'Anzac' stand for?

Understanding

3 Write down what is the same about Zac's grandpa and great-great-grandpa and what is different.

4 Explain why Zac thinks his grandpa is a hero.

5 What is Zac's grandpa's legacy?

Applying

6 Trace a simple world map. Find and label Vietnam, Turkey and Gallipoli.

7 Research and write about what happened on 25 April 1915 when the soldiers landed at Gallipoli.

Analysing

8 Draw a picture of Grandpa's medals. Explain why you think Grandma says the medals are getting too heavy for her.

Evaluating

9 List the reasons why you think 'I won't forget' is a good title or a bad title. Write two new titles.

Creating

10 Write a poem about Anzac Day. Illustrate your poem and present it to the class.

How to organise a Harmony Day celebration

On Harmony Day, we celebrate the traditions of everyone in Australia. Some people were born here. Some came from other countries. Some of our traditions are the same and others are different. Together we share these traditions. They are part of the Australian way of life.

So, let's celebrate with a Harmony Day lunch!

Aims

- To plan and hold a great Harmony Day lunch
- To include everyone in the class

1 Plan

Have a class meeting to **organise** the lunch.

- Talk about your **aims**.
- Choose a date.
- Talk about what to wear – orange or traditional clothes.
- Divide the class into teams – food, artwork, place.
- Choose team leaders.
- Make a list of people to invite, besides the class.

2 Food team

- Talk about the menu – food from different countries.
- Decide which families you will ask to cook each dish.
- List what you need – cups, plates and so on.

organise do what is needed to hold an event
aims goals that you work towards

Students and their families celebrate Harmony Day.

3 Artwork team

- Brainstorm ideas for decorations.
- Design invitations.
- List what you need – paper, paints and so on.

4 Place team

- Decide where to have the lunch.
- List what you need – tables, chairs and so on.
- Draw a site plan showing where to put the food tables and where people will sit.

Present your plan to the class.

Breakaway tasks

Remembering

1 List the aims in your own words.
2 Write down three things that need to be planned.

Understanding

3 Why do you think everyone in the class needs to come?
4 Draw the site plan from point 4 of the plan.

Applying

5 Research and write about how Harmony Day is celebrated in Australia.
6 Write two names for the Harmony Day lunch.

Analysing

7 Design the invitation to the Harmony Day lunch. Decide what information you need to include on the invitation.

Evaluating

8 With a partner, talk about whether the plan covers everything you need to do to organise the lunch. Add anything that you think is missing and list all the points in order.

Creating

9 Create a timetable so that everything is ready in time for Harmony Day.
10 Write and present a song about Harmony Day for the lunch guests.

The Lion Drummer

The Lion Drummer, by Gabrielle Wang, is about a girl called Lulu who dreams that one day she will be the lion drummer in the Chinese dragon parade. Here, she watches the dragon parade with her *baba* (father).

We live in Chinatown, so we don't have to go far to see the dragon parade. There are lots of people in the street. We find a place to stand on the edge of the road.

Soon I hear drumming and the crash of **cymbals**.

At the top of the street I see a person wearing a huge ***papier mâché*** head with a smiley face.

"Who's that funny man, Baba?"

cymbals round brass plates that are hit against each other to make a musical sound

papier mâché torn-up paper mixed with glue used to make models, masks and so on

"He's the monk," Baba says. "He teases the lion and gets him excited. Look, there's the lion now."

Behind the monk, a lion leaps through the archway of Chinatown. He throws his head from side to side and moves his eyes about. He looks so fierce. If I didn't know there were people inside him, I would think he was alive!

Then I see the lion drummer with a big black drum. He's wearing a red headband and is old, but very strong. Another man is pushing him on a platform. The drummer's short drumsticks move so fast they are just a blur.

My heart starts racing. I can feel the rhythm way down in the pit of my stomach as if the drum is inside me.

Breakaway tasks

Remembering

1 Why don't they have to go far to see the dragon parade?

2 Who teases the lion?

3 Make a drawing of the lion drummer.

Understanding

4 Do you think the writer likes the drums? Why?

5 How do you know the lion looks real? Write down your ideas.

Applying

6 Write five adjectives to describe the lion. Use the adjectives to write your own description of the lion.

Analysing

7 Make a simple mask of the monk's head using cardboard and felt pens.

8 Research a dragon parade and draw the dragon.

Evaluating

9 Who would you like to be in the dragon parade? List two reasons why.

Creating

10 Create a musical beat for the drummer and perform it for the class.

Strands in action

Core tasks

1 Plan a NAIDOC Week celebration following the plan for the Harmony Day lunch.
   a Give your event a name and make a poster about it.
   b Write an advertisement for your local newspaper.

2 Write a magazine article about an event celebrated in Australia that came from another country.
   a Find out about your event. Write:
      - an opening paragraph to present your topic
      - a middle paragraph to present the information
      - the last paragraph to sum it up.
   b Draw a picture or find a photo for your article.
   c Present it to the class.

Extra tasks

1 Interview your family or friends about food. Do they eat and cook food from different countries?

2 Write a haiku about an Australian celebration.

3 Make a flag for Harmony Day. Include symbols to show where Australians have come from.

4 Research and write about an Aboriginal and Torres Strait Islander celebration.

Editing or checking your work is an important part of writing. Editing is not just about punctuation and spelling. It's also about the words you choose. Don't use the same words all the time. Use a thesaurus to find different words.